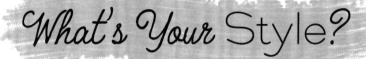

What's Your Style?

EDGY
FASHION

AMANDA ST JOHN

Lerner Publications Company
Minneapolis

Lerner Publications Company
A division of Lerner Publishing Group, Inc.
241 First Avenue North
Minneapolis, MN 55401 U.S.A.

For reading levels and more information, look up this title at www.lernerbooks.com.

Credits: Amy Fitzgerald and Sara E. Hoffmann (editorial), Emily Harris (design), Giliane Mansfeldt (photos), Heidi Hogg (production).

Main body text set in Adrianna Light 12/14.
Typeface provided by Chank.

Library of Congress Cataloging-in-Publication Data

StJohn, Amanda, 1982-
    Edgy fashion / by Amanda StJohn ; illustrated by Ashley Newsome Kubley
        pages cm. — (What's your style?)
    Includes index.
    ISBN 978-1-4677-1468-6 (lib. bdg. : alk. paper)
    ISBN 978-1-4677-2527-9 (eBook)
    1. Fashion. 2. Girls' clothing. 3. Preteens—Clothing. 4. Beauty, Personal.
I. Kubley, Ashley Newsome, ill. II. Title.
TT562.S78 2014
646.4'06—dc23   2013013595

Manufactured in the United States of America
1 – PC – 12/31/13

What's Your Style?

CONTENTS

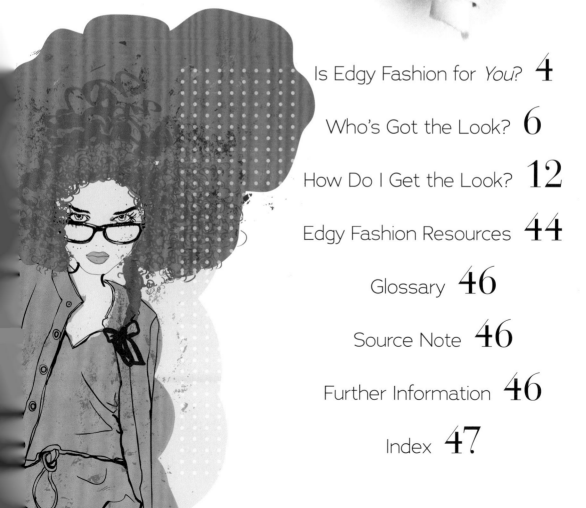

Is **EDGY** FASHION for *You*?

Is edgy fashion up your alley? To find out, grab a pen and paper and record your answers to this style quiz!

1. What color or colors do you usually wear?
   a. white
   b. mellow pastels
   c. bright neons
   d. black

2. You never leave the house without your
   a. braided headband
   b. snapback hat
   c. plaid shirt
   d. creeper shoes

3. When it comes to spicing up your clothes, you add
   a. silk flowers
   b. sequins
   c. wooden beads
   d. studs or zippers

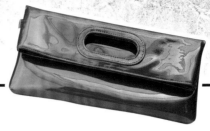

4. If you could save up for a splurge, what would be your ultimate fashion statement?
   a. vintage brand-name T-shirt
   b. pearl necklace
   c. fur coat
   d. leather jacket

5. When you choose an outfit, you want it to
   a. be shocking enough to grab everyone's attention
   b. match what your friends are wearing
   c. seem perfectly put together
   d. be original but not too flashy

6. Where do you find clothes for a new look?
   a. department stores
   b. thrift stores
   c. at home! Old clothes can be transformed.
   d. all of the above

If you answered mostly *d*'s, you're all about the **edgy look**. Edgy fashion is feisty, rebellious, and sophisticated. It makes a statement without shouting. The look is natural—never primly overdone—but it also **embraces the unexpected**.

If you didn't get many *d*'s, edgy might not be for you. But learning about different looks can still be helpful as you create your own unique style. Read on to explore the secrets of edgy fashion.

Who's Got
THE LOOK?

The best way to start learning about edgy style is to check out what others are doing. Take a look at some of the celebrities who've made edgy fashion a phenomenon. They're always putting new spins on a classic look to stay one step ahead of the crowd.

KATE MOSS

In the early 1990s, this British supermodel pioneered the edgy look. She was among the first celebrities to keep her shoulder-length hair loose, with little styling. She wears little or no makeup and keeps accessories to a minimum. As for her clothes, she's often been seen in

- leather jackets over scoop-neck T-shirts;

- skinny jeans with boots; and

- nude makeup with intense eyes and high-shine lip gloss.

Creative Journal— Edgy Style!

Turn an extra notebook into an edgy fashion journal. Glue in all your favorite edgy celebrity photos and news clippings. Then take notes and sketch your own fashion ideas.

Madonna's teenage daughter has been on the edgy fashion scene since she was thirteen. Lourdes's most dramatic style statement came in 2012 when she partially shaved her head.

Lourdes (right) hits the town with mom Madonna (left).

In addition to her bold haircut, other elements of Lourdes's look include

- studded leather jackets;
- black jeans with studded pockets; and
- cutoff denim shorts.

Lourdes rocks a leather jacket with a wide range of edgy outfits.

Like Lourdes, this British recording artist sweeps her long, wavy hair over a partially shaved head. For her overall look, Cher mixes edgy elements with a feminine style—creating an image that's truly fierce. She's been spotted wearing

- a black quilted biker jacket;

- a stud rib cardigan;

- black tights and leggings;

- black boots; and

- a pendant necklace.

For Cher, no two edgy looks are alike!

This musical superstar is always on the cutting edge of fashion. In 2012 Rhianna shaved a patch of her hair and swept her long locks forward. She wears understated, edgy makeup but often adds a strong pop of glamorous lip color. Some of her other edgy looks feature

- little black dresses;

- skinny jeans with zippers on the calves; and

- black boots with tassels.

KRISTEN STEWART

Ever since starring in *Twilight*, this actress has been on the edgy fashion map. She follows Kate Moss's lead when it comes to natural-looking hair and subtle makeup. Her go-to accessories include dark bracelets and pendant necklaces. On the clothing front, you might catch her rocking

* little black dresses;

* black jackets and T-shirts; and

* formfitting black pants with sleek black boots or sandals.

How Do I
GET THE LOOK?

Are you ready to make your own edgy style statements? You can get started right away. The "edge" in edgy fashion is all about sensing a new trend ahead of everyone else— and expressing your individuality without worrying what others think. Still, it's always useful to know the basics. Here are some tips to consider as you start building your edgy wardrobe.

BRING ON THE BLACK

Black flatters any body type. It's quiet yet dramatic. Of course, wearing too much black can look gloomy, so incorporate subtle splashes of color. For Kristen Stewart, a black dress with patches of blue on the sleeves and pockets does the trick. Lourdes Leon offsets a dark ensemble by wearing a colored shirt under her black jacket.

A white hat can brighten up your look.

sloppy

sleek

DON'T DO TOO MUCH

An edgy girl keeps it real by not going overboard. Limit your layers. You don't need to wear three different tops under your jacket. That extra bulk is distracting—not to mention uncomfortable! Don't get carried away with embellishments either. If your outfit is slashed *and* zippered *and* studded, your sleek look becomes sloppy.

The **Bright** Side of Blending In

When asked why she wore so much black and gray, Kate Moss responded that it bores the paparazzi and keeps them at bay. Dressing edgily is about being comfortable and genuine, not about getting attention.

LOVE YOUR LEGS

Find legwear that's formfitting from hip to ankle. Nothing should be so tight that it's uncomfortable, but a streamlined silhouette creates structure in your look.

Your legwear can add a pop of color to an otherwise all-black outfit.

Edgy Influences

Teenagers in the United Kingdom and the United States used to dress like mirror images of their parents. How boring is that? But by the 1950s, teens had rebelled. Inspired by rock 'n' roll music, they created daring new looks. Girls who knew how to sew made their own clothing whenever possible for maximum originality. Today's edgy fashion echoes the fierce style of the '50s.

Hollywood heartthrob James Dean helped inspire the edgy look.

MIX CASUAL AND FASHION-FORWARD PIECES

Your overall look should be lived-in, comfortable, and expressive of *you*. So choose signature items—your favorite studded bracelet, your lucky jacket, or your comfy boots—to wear almost every day. Build on that basic style with new, creative elements no one's expecting. Showcase a new piece of clothing or a unique, surprising piece of jewelry against the backdrop of your familiar look.

Now that you've learned the fundamentals, it's time to start stocking your closet. Take a look at the core edgy items you'll need.

CLOTHING

LEATHER JACKET

An edgy jacket looks like a boyish motorcycle jacket. It doesn't need to be real leather, as long as it's black, durable, and formfitting. It should be waist length to hip length and fit you "just right," especially in the shoulders and arms. You need only one, so it's worthwhile to invest in a material and cut that you love.

Leather Is Forever

How did the leather jacket become forever linked with the rebel image? Thank the stars of the '50s. Free-spirited singer Elvis Presley made it part of his look, and tough-guy actors like Marlon Brando and James Dean sported it too.

Marlon Brando lived on the edge . . . and loved his leather.

PLAIN BLACK T-SHIRT

A chill black T-shirt is comfortable and inexpensive, and you can customize it to your heart's content. But don't hesitate to mix things up sometimes with gray, ivory, or even white T's—not to mention your favorite band T-shirts.

SKINNY JEANS

Tapered jeans fit snugly all the way to your ankle, with no extra fabric to blur your figure. This contrasts with your loose T-shirts and baggy sweaters to create a balanced look.

LITTLE

BLACK

DRESS

Pick simple dresses without much frill. Go for a cut that falls above the knee. You don't always have to aim for a night-on-the-town vibe. Casual shirtdresses or tunics make classy everyday outfits.

BLACK LEGGINGS

If you were wondering what to wear with those little black dresses, look no further. Textured black tights work too! Don't shred your legwear. Stick with a clean, sophisticated look.

Most leggings stop at the ankle, giving you plenty of freedom in your footwear choices.

CUTOFF DENIM SHORTS

All that black can get hot in the summer! Cutoffs let your legs breathe. A few rips and frays add a lived-in look—but no need to pay extra for denim that's already distressed. If you can't wait for ordinary wear-and-tear to do its work, check with your parents about using sandpaper and scissors to speed up the process.

LONG, SLOUCHY KNIT SWEATERS

When the weather turns cold, swap that thin T-shirt for something heavier. Paired with skinny jeans or leggings, an oversized sweater softens your profile without turning you into a shapeless lump.

One Girl's Trash, Another Girl's Treasure

Even Kate Moss is a fan of finding unique pieces on the cheap. "I used to just go to [rummage] sales and have bags and bags of clothes," she says, "and then the stylists would use them on shoots."

Leggings— Seamed Stocking Style

Refresh your leggings by adding zippers.

What you need:

- 1 pair of ankle-length leggings

- a ruler

- chalk

- 2 14-inch (35.5-centimeter) zippers

- scissors

- a scrap of cardboard

- fabric glue

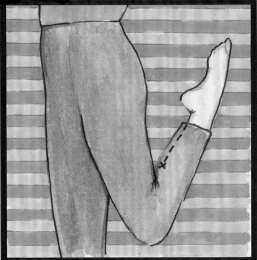

What you do:

1. Starting at the ankle, use a ruler to draw a 14-inch chalk line straight up the back of one leg on your pair of leggings.. Hold one of the zippers to the line. The zipper slide should be lined up with the bottom of the leg. Draw a stop mark at the top of the zipper. Repeat this process on the other leg.

2. Cut along the lines without going past your stop marks.

3. Slide a piece of cardboard inside one leg. This will prevent you from accidentally gluing the fabric together. Then grab a zipped zipper by the side opposite the zipper slide. Dab fabric glue on the fabric ends. Slip the glued ends inside your legging at the top of your cut, and press them together for a few seconds to anchor the zipper.

4. Unzip your zipper. Put a strip of glue along the fabric part of one of the upper halves. Working toward the ankle, press the fabric of your legging against the zipper and glue until fully attached. Repeat on the other side with the zipper's other half. Do not cut off the extra zipper tape.

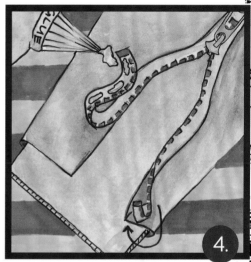

5. Two tabs of zipper tape should be sticking out. Place a little glue on one. Fold it over the hem, and hold it down for a few seconds. Repeat this process until both tabs are glued.

6. Repeat steps 3 to 5 on the other leg.

After letting your leggings dry, zip them and try them on. Your altered leggings will look cute with a little black dress and sandals. Stud the exposed zipper tabs if you like.

SHOES

Edgy style is a natural choice for shoe lovers. When legwear takes a backseat, your shoes step into the spotlight.

BOOTS

Get that "urban girl" edge with black boots. Wear them with your little black dress. You can go for a lace-up work boot or a mid-calf fashion boot. A slouchy boot adds texture and relaxes your look. A flat-soled boot will be a healthier choice for your feet if you wear boots every day.

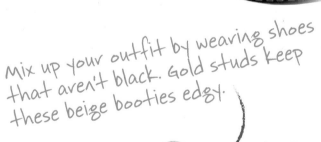

Mix up your outfit by wearing shoes that aren't black. Gold studs keep these beige booties edgy.

CREEPER SHOES

Have you seen these on Rihanna? Designed in the 1950s, the creeper features a thick rubber sole with rippled edging. Today, they're back as one of the hottest trends in footwear. Find them with single-, double-, and triple-thick soles. Wear them with anything in your closet.

SHOE BOOTIES AND HEELS

You can find these kinds of footwear in almost any material. Imitation leather, velvet, and suede are especially chic. Add flourish and contrast with embellishments. Tassels are hot lately. So are grommets, studs, and zippers. You can also make a statement with a bold color of your choice.

studded shoe

Stunning Studded Shoes

Edgy style demands uniqueness, but one-of-a-kind items are costly to buy. It's much cheaper—and more authentic—to personalize basic footwear with your own studded designs.

What you need:

- pencil and paper (optional)

- metal studs (found in most arts and craft stores or online)

- an awl

- pliers or another tool to flatten the studs

What you do:

1. Think about the design you want to make. You can browse celebrity shoes for ideas. If it helps, sketch your idea before getting started.

2. The back of a stud has sharp prongs that can be pushed through most shoes. If your shoes are thick, don't force the studs. Instead, gently press a stud into the shoe to make a mark. Then, with help from an adult, use the awl to make holes.

3. Once you've pushed your studs through the holes, use the side of a pair of pliers to fold the prongs. This protects your fingers from puncture wounds!

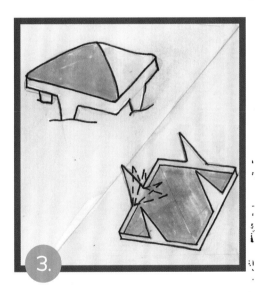

ACCESSORIES

Many edgy accessories can—and should—be customized. Embrace your creativity by making your own accessories when possible.

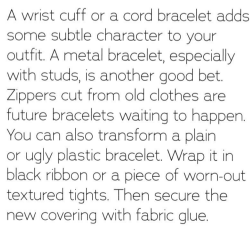

ARMOR FOR YOUR ARMS

A wrist cuff or a cord bracelet adds some subtle character to your outfit. A metal bracelet, especially with studs, is another good bet. Zippers cut from old clothes are future bracelets waiting to happen. You can also transform a plain or ugly plastic bracelet. Wrap it in black ribbon or a piece of worn-out textured tights. Then secure the new covering with fabric glue.

HEADGEAR

Nothing says "living on the edge" like a black fedora. A single-color knit stocking cap works too. Keep your hats comfortable, simple, and just a little sassy.

SUNGLASSES

Shades with wide lenses harken back to the flyboys of World War II (1939–1945) and the free spirits of the 1960s. With brand names like Aviator and Wayfarer, they still give off a rebellious, adventurous vibe.

PENDANTS

Long chains and pendant necklaces energize your outfit. Pendants are easy to make. Just add a charm in the shape of a symbol you love—such as a butterfly or a rosebud—to a chain or a length of cord. Flaunt a flirty look by slipping a black tassel on a cord. Or get fierce with a guitar pick slung on a metal chain. Cher Lloyd adores her skull and tusk pendant, and she layers necklaces together for extra effect.

BELTS

Your long shirts, tunic sweaters, and dresses go from slouchy to snazzy when you add a belt. Belts with studs or decorative buckles add a dash of pizazz.

Metal Studs

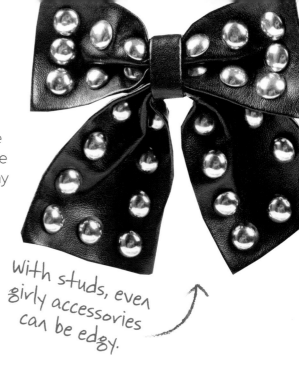

These bits of bling bring a dose of toughness *and* a little sparkle to an outfit. They come in many styles, including round, cone-shaped, and pyramid-shaped.

With studs, even girly accessories can be edgy.

Zippers

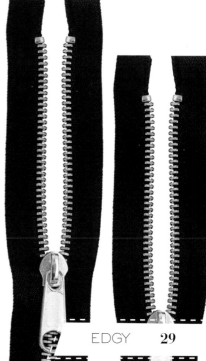

Chunky zippers, skinny zippers, zippers on your clothes, zippers on your boots—they're a constant in edgy fashion, and they can be used in countless ways.

Zippy Chain Earrings

These statement earrings add shine around your cheek and neck. Ditch your necklaces when wearing them.

What you need:

- 2 zipper pulls (These cost about 25 cents apiece. But you can cut them off discarded clothes too.)

- a 9-inch (23 cm) lightweight chain with a gold, silver, or brassy finish

- 2 jump rings (metal rings used to make chains or jewelry), plus a couple of extras just in case

- pliers

- a ruler

- wire cutters

- 2 earring posts with loops

What you do:

1. The top of your zipper pull has a divider in it. Slip your chain around it. Add a jump ring to the end of your chain, and attach it snugly to the main chain. Use pliers to close the jump ring. Add the second zipper pull to the opposite end of your chain.

2. Use wire cutters to snip the chain 2 inches (5 cm) above each zipper.

3. Open the little loop on your earring post sideways. Slip the last link of your chain in, and close the loop. *Voilà!*

Add the Funk

Try this: Make one earring exactly as directed in the Styling DIY, but change up the second. Attach the chain to the post loop and let it dangle. Have an adult use a hot glue gun to attach the zipper pull to the earring post.

Hair and Makeup

Edgy hair and makeup often look like no-brainers, but they offer plenty of ways to get creative and show off your own style.

A little mascara goes a long way.

Less Is More

You don't need makeup to be edgy. Kate Moss often goes without it. If you do wear makeup, follow her lead and stick to an understated look. A nude face with subtle upper-eye mascara is enough for Kate.

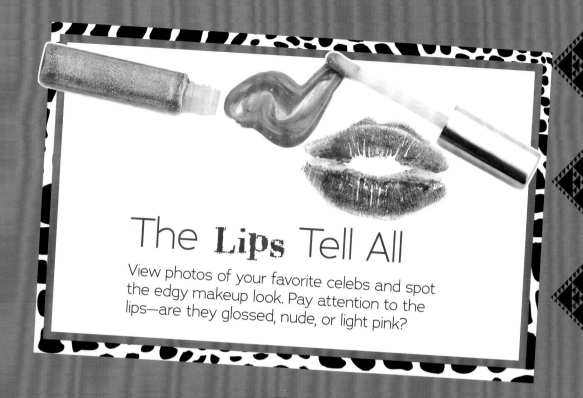

The **Lips** Tell All

View photos of your favorite celebs and spot the edgy makeup look. Pay attention to the lips—are they glossed, nude, or light pink?

Kristen balances her dramatic eye makeup with sheer lip gloss.

MAKE A STATEMENT

On the other hand, you can add an extra cosmetic touch to highlight a particular feature. Rihanna plays with her edgy look by pumping up her lip color. Cher Lloyd emphasizes her eyes with three layers of fake eyelashes, while Kristen Stewart favors smoky eye shadow. Avoid overload by playing up just one element at a time—eyes or lips, for instance, but not both at once.

Cat Eye

If you're allowed to wear makeup and want to add some edge to your eyes, give this look a try.

What you need:

• black liquid eyeliner with a felt tip

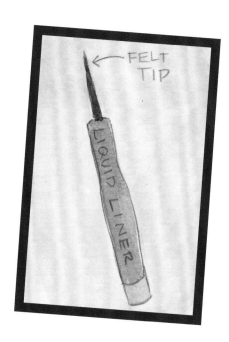

What you do:

1. Brace your hand against your cheek and your elbow against a countertop. Tilt your head back. Starting at the inner corner of your upper eyelid, use short strokes to apply the eyeliner. This prevents your skin from bunching and causing skip marks. Keep your eyeliner right against your lash line. A gap between your eyelashes and the makeup will look unfinished.

2. When you reach the outer corner of your eye, it's time to "wing out" the liner. Make a tiny dot slightly above your eye, about even with the end of your eyebrow. Draw an angled line connecting your upper eyelid to this dot.

3. Draw another line connecting the dot to your bottom waterline (the inner rim of your lower lid). Fill in the narrow gap between the two lines to complete the wing. You can also shade the rest of your waterline, or you can leave it makeup-free.

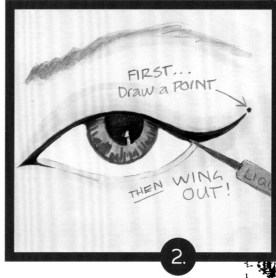

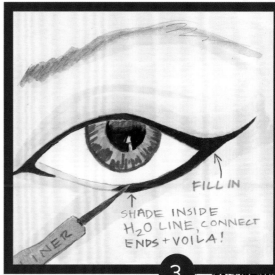

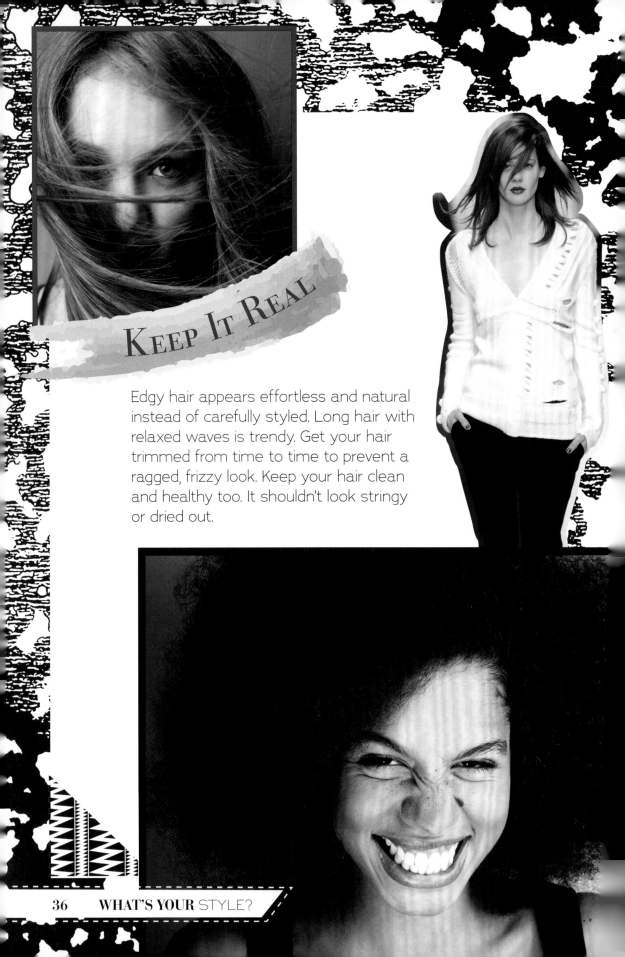

KEEP IT REAL

Edgy hair appears effortless and natural instead of carefully styled. Long hair with relaxed waves is trendy. Get your hair trimmed from time to time to prevent a ragged, frizzy look. Keep your hair clean and healthy too. It shouldn't look stringy or dried out.

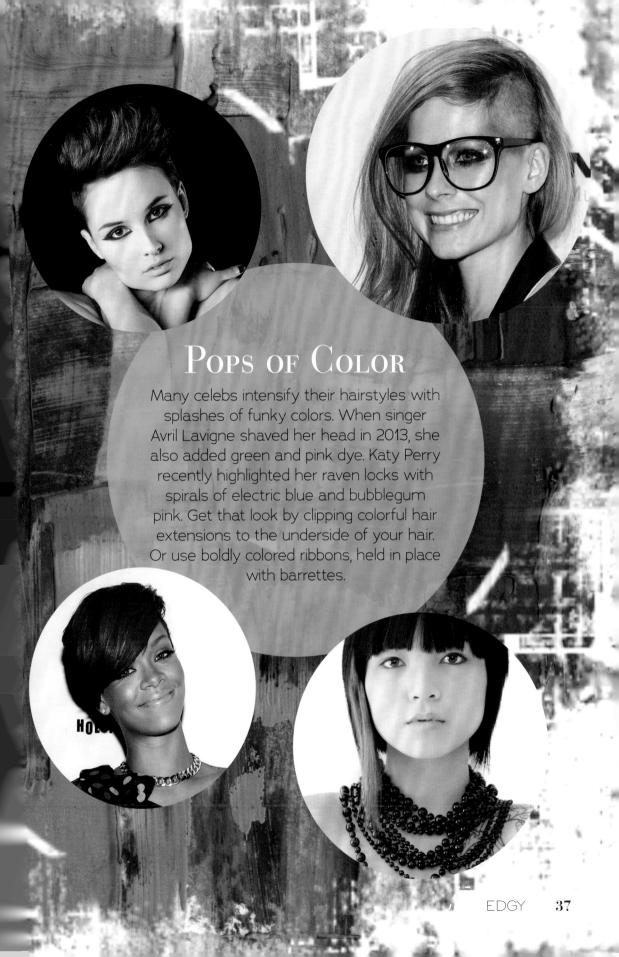

Pops of Color

Many celebs intensify their hairstyles with splashes of funky colors. When singer Avril Lavigne shaved her head in 2013, she also added green and pink dye. Katy Perry recently highlighted her raven locks with spirals of electric blue and bubblegum pink. Get that look by clipping colorful hair extensions to the underside of your hair. Or use boldly colored ribbons, held in place with barrettes.

THE SHAVED LOOK

Wilder hairstyles are also hot with the edgy crowd. Lourdes Leon, Rihanna, and Avril Lavigne have all sported partially shaved heads recently. Dying to try this? Check with your parents. If they're okay with it, next time you get a haircut, bring along a picture of the shaved look you want. Show it to your stylist before he or she goes to work. To get the edge of this look without resorting to a razor, add just a few cornrows on one side of your head and voluminous curls everywhere else.

SHORT & SWEET

Over the last couple of years, Rihanna's sported a variety of bobs and cropped hairstyles. These short, casual haircuts are often asymmetrical, looking different from every angle. This type of haircut shows off your neck and frames your face. It works for a variety of face shapes, hair types, and natural hair colors. Plus, it looks great with your edgy jacket. Use a curling iron to add volume and glamour, or try a flat iron for something fiery.

Styling DIY:

Tousled Rock Hairstyle

Prep this super-simple updo before bed and wake up with an effortless edge!

What you need:

- a claw-style hair clip or bobby pins

- volumizing foam (optional)

- hair spray (optional)

What you do:

1. If your hair has been freshly washed, partially dry it. Add a bit of volumizing foam if you'd like and work it in with your fingers.

2. Twist your hair up on top of your head. Use a claw clip or pins to hold it in place. After your hair has dried, spritz with hair spray if you desire to make sure it stays in place while you sleep.

3. In the morning, take the clip out and lightly fluff your hair into place. Don't comb or brush it. Let your hair be loose and natural.

Your Edgy Look

Rebellious, hip, radical, and fun, edgy fashion will always be hot. But don't wait for the newest trends to find you. Get out there and experiment. Maybe you'll transform your wardrobe with studs and zippers. Maybe you'll freshen up your look with a quirky new piece or find inventive ways to wear old clothes. No matter what, it's up to you to create your own unique style. Rock on, fashionista!

Keep it classically formfitting, or dare to loosen up!

The right accessory—like a signature pair of shades—works with any outfit.

What stands out to you about these edgy ensembles?

EDGY FASHION RESOURCES

Where to Find Edgy Items

- Visit thrift stores, local flea markets, and garage sales to find jeans, jackets, and other clothing basics.

- Look in fabric stores, craft stores, and bead shops for studs, zippers, tassels, jewelry, and other art and sewing supplies.

- Check your favorite retail websites—or a crafty site—for all of the above! (When looking for studs, use keywords such as *metal studs* or *pyramid studs* for the best online search results.)

Is your edgy style dressed down or dressed up?

You can find unique fashion treasures wherever you look.

Studs come in all shapes. These are pyramids.

Songs to Inspire Your Edgy Fashionista

"Firework" by Katy Perry

"Gold Lion" by Yeah Yeah Yeahs

"Let Go" by Avril Lavigne

"Marchin On" by OneRepublic

"Right Now" by Rihanna

"Stop Crying Your Heart Out" by Oasis

Glossary

awl: a small spike used to create holes. A stitching awl is especially useful for puncturing leather.

fashionista: a person devoted to fashion

grommet: a small metal, plastic, or rubber ring that helps to hold open a hole that you've intentionally made in a piece of fabric

jump ring: a metal ring used to make chains or jewelry

rebel: a person who resists control or tradition

waterline: the inner rim of your lower eyelid

Source Note

19. Amy Larocca, "I Am a Woman Now," *New York Magazine*, February 15, 2009, http://nymag.com/fashion/09/spring/54319.

Further Information

Corfee, Stephanie. *Fashion Design Workshop: Stylish Step-by-Step Projects and Drawing Tips for Up-and-Coming Designers.* Irvine, CA: Walter Foster, 2012.
Express your personal style through fashion design drawings.

Edge, Laura B. *From Jazz Babies to Generation Next: The History of the American Teenager.* Minneapolis: Twenty-First Century Books, 2011.
Where does that desire to express yourself come from? Find out here.

Girls' Life
http://www.girlslife.com/category/fashion.aspx
This just may be the number one magazine for girls ages ten to fifteen. Check out the fashion section for trends, tips, and more.

Seventeen
http://www.seventeen.com
Connect with *Seventeen* magazine online to access celebrity profiles, hair and beauty tips, and more.

Shoket, Ann. *Seventeen Ultimate Guide to Style: How to Find Your Perfect Look.* **Philadelphia: Running Press, 2011.**
This book offers another take on the edgy look—and an introduction to other styles that might catch your eye.

Stalder, Erika. *Fashion 101: A Crash Course in Clothing.* **San Francisco: Zest Books, 2008.**
This fun, illustrated book gives you the must-know basics about clothes and how to wear them.

Teen Vogue
http://www.teenvogue.com
This is your go-to site for teen style, culture, and fashion.

Thomas, Isabel. *Being a Fashion Stylist.* **Minneapolis: Lerner Publications Company, 2013.**
Ever wondered what it's like to work as a fashion stylist? Get an inside peek at this exciting career.

INDEX

PHOTO ACKNOWLEDGMENTS

The images in this book are used with the permission of: © Alexkar08/Bigstock, pp. 2, 28; © Yusuf Doganay/Shutterstock, p. 3 (inset); © Ppart/Bigstock, p. 4 (top); © Todd Strand/Independent Picture Service, pp. 4 (bottom), 17 (bottom right), 17 (bottom middle), 19 (bottom left), 26 (middle left); © HannaMariah/Bigstock, p. 5 (top); © Miromiro/Bigstock, p. 5 (bottom); KPF/ZWP WENN Photos/Newscom, p. 6 (left); © Venturelli/WireImage/Getty Images, p. 6 (right); © Miquel Benitez/WireImage/Getty Images, p. 7 (right); © Alex Moss/FilmMagic/Getty Images, p. 7 (left); © Kevin Mazur/Getty Images, pp. 8 (top left), 11 (bottom left), 39 (middle); © George Napolitano/FilmMagic/Getty Images, p. 8 (top left); infusny-160/Elder-Ordonez/INFphoto.com/Newscom, p. 8 (bottom); © Frederick M. Brown/Getty Images, p. 9 (top); © Tim Whitby/Getty Images, p. 9 (bottom left); © Jamie McCarthy/Getty Images, p. 9 (bottom middle); © Jason LaVeris/FilmMagic/Getty Images, pp. 9 (bottom right), 11 (top); © Neil Mockford/FilmMagic/Getty Images, p. 10 (top); © Jason Merritt/Getty Images, p. 10 (bottom left); © NCP/Star Max/FilmMagic/Getty Images, p. 10 (bottom right); © Larry Busacca/Getty Images, p. 11 (bottom right); © Anton Oparin/Shutterstock, pp. 12, 15 (bottom left), 42 (right); © Jelena Ivanovic/Dreamstime, p. 13 (top left); © Image Source/Getty Images, p. 13 (top right); © Stuart Wilson/Getty Images, p. 13 (bottom); © Anna Kostina/Dreamstime, p. 14 (right); © iStockphoto/Saime Deniz Tuyel Dogan, p. 14 (top right); © iStockphoto/Juan Carlos Rodriguez, p. 14 (bottom right); © John Kobal Foundation/Moviepix/Hulton Archive/Getty Images, p. 15 (top); © Nata Sha/Shutterstock, p. 15 (bottom right); © Karkas/Bigstock, p. 16 (top); © Columbia Pictures/Album/SuperStock, p. 16 (bottom); © iStockphoto/clu, p. 17 (top left); © iStockphoto/Peeterv, p. 17 (top right); © Szefei/Dreamstime, pp. 17 (bottom left), 43 (bottom left); © yganko/Bigstock, p. 18 (left); © iStockphoto/Dendong, p. 18 (top left); © Mates/Bigstock, p. 18 (top middle); © Gordana Sermek/Shutterstock, p. 18 (top right); © Denis Aglichev/Dreamstime, p. 18 (bottom); © New Wave/Shutterstock, p. 19 (top left); © PhotoNAN/Shutterstock, p. 19 (top right); © Andrey Armyagov/Bigstock, p. 19 (middle right); © iStockphoto/Thinkstock, pp. 19 (middle left), 22 (top), 33 (top left); © Pascal Le Segretain/WireImage/Getty Images, p. 19 (bottom right); © Coprid/Bigstock, p. 22 (middle); © Olga Mark/Bigstock, p. 22 (bottom left); © iStockphoto/StringerPhotography, p. 22 (bottom right); © Justin Maresch/Shutterstock, p. 23 (top); © Lazar_x/Dreamstime, pp. 23 (middle), 27 (right); © iStockphoto/penguenstok, p. 23 (bottom); p. 28 (top right); © iStockphoto/kyoshino, p. 26 (top right); © Berna Safoglu/Dreamstime, p. 26 (top left); © iStockphoto/dimj, p. 26 (middle right); © iStockphoto/SeanPavonePhoto, p. 26 (center); © Goruppa/Bigstock, p. 26 (bottom right); © iStockphoto/Kate Shephard, p. 26 (bottom left); © Aaron Amat/Bigstock, p. 27 (right top); © iStockphoto/Winterling, p. 27 (right middle); © iStockphoto/Robert Marfin, p. 27 (right bottom); © Desislava Vasileva/Dreamstime, p. 28 (top left); © Bert Folsom/Dreamstime, p. 28 (middle); © iStockphoto/Camilla Wisbauer, p. 28 (bottom left); © iStockphoto/Jessica Morelli, p. 28 (bottom right); © Ronstik/Bigstock, p. 29 (top); © BCFC/Bigstock, p. 29 (bottom); © iStockphoto/GlobalStock, p. 32 (left); © iStockphoto/IndigoBetta, p. 32 (right); © Miskokordic/Bigstock, p. 33 (top right); © Dimitrios Kambouris/Getty Images, p. 33 (bottom); © Lithian/Dreamstime, p. 36 (top left); © Pavel Bendau/Dreamstime, p. 36 (top right); © Djomas/Shutterstock, p. 36 (bottom); © Vasilchenko/Bigstock, p. 37 (top left); © Chelsea Lauren/Getty Images, p. 37; © Christopher Polk/Getty Images, p. 37 (bottom); © Ben Heys/Bigstock, p. 37 (bottom right); © Eyecandy Images/Thinkstock, p. 38 (inset); © iStockphoto/Todor Tsvetkov, p. 38; © Rido81/Bigstock, p. 39 (top); © Image Source RF/Wonwoo Lee/Getty Images, p. 39 (bottom); © Fotowire/Bigstock, p. 42 (left); © iStockphoto/Alexey Tkachenko, p. 43 (top right); © Crystalfoto/Bigstock, p. 43 (top left); © George Pimentel/Getty Images, p. 43 (middle); © Ovidiu Hrubaru/Shutterstock, p. 43 (bottom right),); © iStockphoto/Beba73, pp. 44 (bottom), 44 (right), 44 (left); © cygnusx/Bigstock, p. 45.

Backgrounds: © Svaga/Shutterstock, pp. 1, 49; © Alex Kar08/Bigstock, pp. 2, 28; © Wollertz/Bigstock, p. 3; © Gordan/Bigstock, pp. 4-5, 22-23; © Pokaz/Bigstock, pp. 6-7, 37; © Yih Graphic/Bigstock, pp. 8-9, 15-16, 31; © Lavanda/Bigstock, pp. 10-11; © iStockphoto/Anthony Rosenberg, p. 12; © Eky Studio/Bigstock, pp. 16, 26, 32; © Belinka/Bigstock, pp. 20-21; © kjpargeter/Bigstock, pp. 24-25, 30-31, 34-35, 40-41; © Ruzanna/Bigstock, p. 36; © RedKoala/Bigstock, pp. 42-43; © Kathie Nichols/Bigstock, pp. 44-45; © run4it/Bigstock, pp. 46-47.

Front Cover: © svaga/Shutterstock (triangle texture); © Ruzanna/Bigstock (abstract pattern); © Ronstik/Bigstock (bow tie); © iStockphoto/penguenstok (necklace and shoe); © iStockphoto/Dendong (black dress); © HannaMariah/Bigstock (purse); © yganko/Bigstock (lace); © PhotoNAN/Shutterstock (jean shorts); © Todd Strand/Independent Picture Service (earrings); © iStockphoto/Winterling (sunglasses).

Back Cover: © Eky Studio/Bigstock (background); © Ppart/Bigstock (shoes); © Coprid/Bigstock (boots); © Todd Strand/Independent Picture Service (pants).